BEHIND

THE

LEGEND

 little bee books

An imprint of Bonnier Publishing USA
251 Park Avenue South, New York, NY 10010
Copyright © 2018 by Bonnier Publishing USA
All rights reserved, including the right of reproduction in whole or in part in any form.
Little Bee Books is a trademark of Bonnier Publishing USA, and associated colophon is a trademark of Bonnier Publishing USA.
Manufactured in the United States LAK 0118

Library of Congress Cataloging-in-Publication Data is available upon request

ISBN: 978-1-4998-0571-0 (pbk)
First Edition 10 9 8 7 6 5 4 3 2 1
978-1-4998-0572-7 (hc)
First Edition 10 9 8 7 6 5 4 3 2 1

littlebeebooks.com
bonnierpublishingusa.com

DRAGONS

by Erin Peabody

art by Victor Rivas

little bee books

CONTENTS

MEET THE MONSTER

"Come not between the dragon and his wrath."
— William Shakespeare, *King Lear*

With its abundant leathery scales, spooky bat-like wings, and blowtorch of a mouth, the dragon is one of our most legendary monsters. No creature has been depicted more across world cultures than this mammoth reptile whose breath is typically considered as heinous as its deeds.

The dragon is all scary monsters combined. The ultimate portrait of creepy, dragons may possess glowing-ember eyes; dewy, scaled skin; poisonous breath; membrane-thin wings; and a stinging arrow tip of a tail. One ancient legend even features a winged dragon that dribbles toxic urine from the sky!

Of course, modern books, movies, and music remind us that dragons can also be good-hearted, protective, silly, funny—even adorable! (Think Toothless from *How to Train Your Dragon*, Mushu from Disney's *Mulan*, or the song "Puff, the Magic Dragon," about lovable Puff and his onetime kid pal, Jackie Paper.)

These characters are only the tip of the iceberg (or dragon's tail) when it comes to giant, flame-shooting reptiles, though. The complete story of dragons, you'll soon find out, goes WAAAAAY back—back to the dawning of the world's earliest religions and civilizations. The famous thirteenth-century Italian explorer Marco Polo was convinced he saw dragons in China. (Of course, he also claimed to see creatures that were part-man, part-dog!) The Christian and Hebrew bibles reference dragons. Ancient Greeks and Romans spun clever (and oftentimes ridiculous!) tales about the scaly beasts.

Over thousands of years, tales of fire-breathing, flying terrors have rocked our world. Their powerful stories certainly endure—but what of the creatures themselves? Is there *really* such a thing as a dragon—or was there ever? If we could somehow ask a typical eighteenth-century villager this question, the answer would almost certainly be a trembling, quivering, but resounding, yes. Up through the 1700s, people fervently feared these fire-eating reptiles that allegedly scorched entire crops and villages.

Even today, every now and then, there are reports of bizarre, scaled creatures that remind witnesses of serpents or dragons. One such alleged beast, the Tatzelwurm (German for "clawed worm"),

still makes the occasional observer shudder and shriek. First documented in 1779, the allegedly fierce and leaping reptile so frightened a man that he died from a heart attack! Reports of this unproven mystery creature, or cryptid, continue today.

Eager for more? Then climb atop your favorite fire-breathing character and hold on tight. We're about to soar back to a time when dragons ruled the earth.

CHAPTER ONE

HOW DRACONIAN!

"Dragons are S-S-SELFISH. . . . Dragons are heartless and
we have no mercy. . . ." —Toothless, in Cressida Cowell's
How to Train Your Dragon

Fire-breather. Dungeon-dweller. Reptile with a bad attitude. These are all good descriptors of the "typical" dragon. No, it's not polite—or even accurate—to stereotype or generalize. Yet there is a familiar dragon from the days of yore: a hideous beast that boasted leathery, impenetrable scales; fiery, knock-'em-dead breath; and talons (claws) that could rip and shred.

Most notably, however, these dragons were EVIL. Common during the medieval period in Europe, these beasts were the very essence of nasty. They were fierce, cunning, and bloodthirsty. They devoured people, children, and pets—popping victims into their smoldering jaws like M&M's. Dragons were heartless, ruthless, and, by one of the most famous accounts in all of history, greedy.

A SCROOGE WITH SCALES

The dragon is so important to human history that one appears in the oldest-known poem in the English language. *Beowulf,* as it's called, was composed by an unknown poet around 700 CE and tells, in part, the story of King Beowulf, who must battle a stingy, gold-hoarding dragon. When someone in the kingdom tiptoes into the dragon's lair and swipes a single gold cup, the attendant dragon (apparently a little touchy) lashes out, unleashing its fiery fury upon all the land.

Caring only for its "hoarded loveliness," this beast starts to "vomit forth fire." Beowulf, unable to stand idly by as his kingdom goes up in smoke, agrees to battle the dragon. With his loyal friend Wiglaf at his side, Beowulf charges at the greedy glutton with his sword, but the weapon simply bounces off the dragon's tough scales. The dragon blows more fire, causing Wiglaf's wooden shield to go up in flames. Then it lunges for Beowulf's neck. Blood spills "in gushing streams." The brave king ultimately succumbs to this irreversible wound, but not before his faithful friend thrusts a perfectly positioned sword into the dragon's soft underbelly.

ALL IN A NAME

Our word *dragon* originates from the Latin word *draco*, which means "huge serpent." And history is filled with many curious "dracos."

There's Draco, the harsh lawmaker from ancient Athens, Greece, best known for his severe (or draconian) punishments. In Roman mythology, the goddess Minerva kills a dragon called Draco. A bright and easily seen constellation in the far northern sky is named Draco. And you might recognize another less-likable one: Draco Malfoy, Harry Potter's antagonist at Hogwarts!

BY GEORGE, I THINK YOU SLAYED IT!

Another of the best-known dragon legends features the pious do-gooder George (history has forgotten his last name), a onetime Roman soldier who lived about 1,700 years ago. George left his army post when he learned that the Roman emperor had ordered all Christians in the region to be killed. So George, the decent guy that he was, chose instead to rove the Middle East, defending his Christian faith.

At that same time, the city of Silene, in Libya, was under siege. A horrible, green-scaled creature with translucent wings and a long, corkscrewing tail was coughing poison on the townspeople's fields and crops. The villagers offered up sheep to satisfy the dragon, a plan that worked splendidly until they ran out of sheep to feed the ravenous beast.

What should we do next? the people wondered. Could a valiant hero step forward to battle the dragon? Could the people devise a scheme—a trap, maybe—by which to ensnare the beast? Could they relocate their town elsewhere? No, no, and, well, no! After convening their brightest minds at a special gathering of the city council, the townsfolk decided that the best way to appease the crop-killing dragon was to feed it . . . children!

Sadly, and horribly, multiple kids were sacrificed. Then the day came when the king's very own daughter was offered up as a piece of dragon kibble. The lovely Alcyone—no doubt wearing her most impressive gown—was tied to a stake at the edge of the swamp where the dragon lived. There, she waited for the monster to sniff her out. But much to her surprise, she was found not only by the dragon, but also by a dashing man atop his gleaming warhorse! It was George!

Not one to waste time, the just-in-the-nick-of-time hero challenged the dragon. He thrust his lance into the creature's neck, mortally wounding it. But the pair needed a way to further confine the creature. That's when Alcyone, like any respectable, medieval maiden, removed her girdle (the sash around her waist) and repurposed it for the task of dragon restraining.

After binding up the dragon with the girdle, George delivered the wounded beast to the king, promising to finish it off if the people in the kingdom converted to Christianity. The king agreed, and George sliced off the dragon's head. For this noble act, George was later made a saint. However, quite unfairly, no special honors were ever given to Alcyone, or to the scores of children who allegedly perished in the tragedy.

DAMSELS AND DRAGONS

Legend says that ladies saw their fair share of dragons, too. But cleverly, these women usually figured out how to tame or destroy the vile creatures using very little effort. Take for instance, Saint Martha of Bethany, a biblical figure from the New Testament. When a scary dragon-like creature called the Tarasque started terrorizing the French countryside—eluding even the best knights—Martha was called in. With a few prayers and hymns, she entranced the dragon, which was later killed by the townspeople. The French city of Tarascon still bears the monster's name.

Another capable dragon fighter was Saint Margaret of Antioch, born around 291 CE. Forced to learn courage the hard way (her mother died when she was young, and her father banished her from her home), Margaret grew up to be a confident young woman. Boldly, she refused to marry a powerful and abusive man in town she was instructed to. But as a woman with few rights (living in a period you might call the "Really Dark Ages"), she was tossed in prison. There, she was forced to confront yet another beast, a real-life, fire-spitting dragon! Swiftly, though, Margaret conquered the dragon with a quick flash of her shiny cross—a trick she should have tried on her earlier bully.

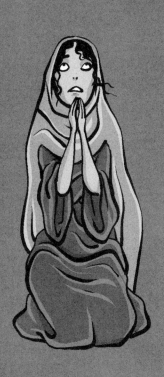

IT WASN'T ALWAYS THIS WAY

So by now, this classic dragon story line must be getting familiar. It includes a dragon symbolizing all that's evil in the world, a heroic soldier, and a maiden who's almost never given a chance to kick dragon butt on her own. Numerous tales follow this formula, including the Greek myth of Perseus and the sea monster/dragon of the god Poseidon, the Scandinavian story about Sigurd and the dragon, and Disney's *Sleeping Beauty*.

But consider this. At one time, dragons and scaled creatures like snakes and serpents were

greatly admired. They were worshiped even. Mexico's ancient Aztecs revered them, and so did the Incas in Peru, who carved serpent symbols into stone. Some Native American tribes considered them so important that they built extensive burial grounds in the shape of snakes, such as the 1,300-foot-long Great Serpent Mound, in Ohio. Snakes play a significant role in many African and Australian folk stories, too. And one of ancient Egypt's most powerful goddesses, Wadjet, was a protective, poison-spitting cobra.

Then something changed. In part, it was the advent of Christianity. Dragons and snakes became vilified and hated. They came to represent greed, temptation, and destruction. The dragon's fiery jaws symbolized the flickering gates of Hell.

Take for instance the well-known serpent that slithers into the Garden of Eden, tempting Eve with the forbidden apple. An enormous and powerful sea creature, Leviathan, is described in the Old Testament as a "twisted serpent" and the "dragon who lives in the sea." When the beast becomes too wild and unruly, it is slain by the archangel Gabriel and then fed to the people. (Dragon buffet, anyone?)

In the next section, we'll learn a little more about why dragons, snakes, and sea serpents were historically clustered together—and how this cold-blooded clan also included deadly leeches and worms!

WHITHER DID THEY SLITHER?

Worms, serpents, snakes, and dragons. In the tales of old, these creatures were all loosely grouped together. If a person caught sight of a strange, slithering, and coiling thing with glistening, scaled skin and a flickering tongue, he or she wasn't likely to stick around for a close-up look! Even if a witness got a decent description, there were no scientific guidebooks back then to help pinpoint what he or she saw.

This lack of scientific knowledge, coupled with a repulsion of all things scaly, slimy, and generally icky, led to a lot of loose name-calling centuries ago. Thus, the terms *dragon*, *serpent*, and *worm* were often used interchangeably. Numerous legends feature one or more of these wriggling villains. And one that still haunts the little village of Washington, England, involves the ever-growing Lambton Worm.

NOT A WEE WORM

The year was 1420, and a young man, John Lambton, was feeling rebellious. He was a lucky lad, an heir to a beautiful English castle, but for whatever reason, John woke up one Sunday morning in a feisty mood. Instead of going to church that day (which EVERYONE pretty much did back then), he decided to go fishing down at the river.

A lovely morning eventually turned into a frustrating afternoon, for John didn't catch a single thing. Feeling rather like a "saddle-goose" (an imbecile) and a "fopdoodle" (a foolish man), John began to curse. Though we don't know what he said, he yelled something improper, and it seemed to trigger a dark and mysterious rippling in the water.

John felt a firm tug on his line, and he started to pull up what appeared to be a large, black worm. He kept reeling, and the worm's head popped up above the water. It had small horns, a bulging brow, and a mouth full of tiny, razor-sharp teeth. Repulsed by this devilish-looking catch, the young man tossed the worm down a nearby well.

Years passed, and John became a noble soldier who fought in the Crusades. He'd outgrown his childish ways. But it seemed something else had grown while John was away. According to an old English folk song:

The worm got fat an' growed and growed
An' growed an aaful size.
He'd greet big teeth, a greet big gob,
An' greet big goggle eyes.

In fact, the worm that John chucked down the well had gotten so big that it became a menace to the whole village. The worm slithered through the countryside, leaving a trail of revolting, searing slime behind it. It could wrap itself around the biggest hill in town—nine times! Massive in size, it preyed on livestock and small children. People were afraid to leave their homes.

WHAT NOW?

And just like the townspeople in the story about Saint George, the citizens of Washington carefully plotted what they should do next. Their creative answer? Feed the worm . . . milk! Surprisingly, the dairy trick worked! The giant worm happily lapped up the large troughs of dairy that people set out for it and continued coming back for more. Yet the local cows could only produce so much milk, so some of the villagers decided to try and battle the worm with swords. But even when they sliced it into pieces, the worm reconnected itself and slithered on.

That's when John Lambton, now a responsible grown-up, returned home. He quickly learned about the whopping worm and knew he must act. He heeded the advice of a wise witch and donned a special suit of metal armor covered in spikes. Her only caveat was this: Once the worm was dead, John would have to kill the next person he saw.

John proceeded to fight the worm. He jabbed at it with his lance, but the thing wrapped itself around him several times, squeezing him tighter and tighter. Then John's armor of protective sharp spikes began to work its magic. The studded outfit punctured the worm in so many places that the writhing creature could not recover.

Gleefully, John rushed to the castle to share his great news, forgetting the one critical detail in the old sage's advice. Now that he had killed the worm, whoever he laid eyes on next must also die. As it turned out, that fatal first glance fell upon his father. But John refused to kill his father. Instead, he would have to endure the worm's bitter curse: For the next nine generations, all heirs to the Lambton estate would die an early death. The witch and the worm weren't kidding about the curse! Allegedly, three generations of Lambton men ended up dying at a young age. One drowned and at least two died in battle. The ninth in line finally wised up. He slept with a horsewhip by his bed, always prepared to defend himself.

CREEPY STATUES WITH A STORY

The French are wonderful weavers of legends. They might be best known for their tales of vicious werewolves: those bloodthirsty night prowlers of long ago thought to have preyed upon shepherds in their fields and babes in their beds. Thanks to those inventors of the beret and the baguette, we can also enjoy a host of thrilling tales about frightful serpent dragons and sea dragons.

We're reminded of one such beast in glancing up at old buildings. Have you ever seen scary, grotesque creatures perched on the ledges of old churches and other historic buildings? With horns, deeply set eyes, and sharp teeth protruding from big jaws, they're called gargoyles. *Gargoyle* comes from the French word *gargouille* and means "gargler." And, sure enough, these weirdos have a dragon history.

Around the seventh century, parts of France were reportedly besieged by water-spouting beasts. Much more powerful than spouting fountains, these dragon-like serpents could seriously spew water. Gushing great waves, gargouilles flooded farmlands and cities. People and animals drowned. In the end, these evil creatures were finally banished by the bishop Romanus of Rouen, who did so by forming his fingers into the shape of a Christian cross. Gargouilles' stone likenesses still endure, though, and can be seen on such famous buildings as France's Notre-Dame cathedral.

BLUSHING BEAST

Another noteworthy French legend concerns a serpent dragon with hideous breath and a funny weakness. Known as a *guivre* (pronounced "geev-ruh"), this creature with a thick, serpentine body and a dragon-like head was thought to inhabit rivers, streams, and other bodies of water—including wells. (For goodness' sake, medieval peeps, don't go near those wells!)

Like other dragons, the guivre also possessed horrible, eye-watering halitosis. But these stinky swimmers took horrid breath to a whole new level. When they blew their putrid mouth fumes on fields, they made crops wither. When they exhaled on villages, they spread deadly plague and disease. And like traditional dragons, they could also skip any snorting and just gobble their victims up!

One day, though, a farmer discovered the beast had an embarrassing shortcoming. After a hard day's work in the hot sun, the farmer shed his sweaty clothes and went for a dip in the local river. To his horror, a guivre popped its head above water nearby. How hideous it appeared, with blazing eyes, devilish horns, and dripping fangs! The man turned and swam away, and as he was naked, happened to "flash" the guivre with his rump. When the man looked back again, he noticed that the sea dragon was no longer

glowering or growling. In fact, it appeared helpless and, of all things, embarrassed. The blushing beastie, apparently scared of nude humans, dove into the water and wasn't seen again.

The French people now had a new weapon with which to buck off the terrible guivre. And so they lived happily—yet, uh . . . nakedly—ever after.

WHEN YOU CROSS A DRAGON WITH A LEECH . . .

. . . you get a dragon leech, one of the most revolting (and awesome!) dragon creatures of all time! And for it, we owe our thanks to the great Passamaquoddy Indian tribe in Maine, whose vibrant people still tell the story.

Long ago, the tribe's most respected medicine man was challenged to a battle by a rival medicine man. Capable of shape-shifting, or turning into other creatures, both shamans used their magic to transform themselves into formidable beasts that duked it out in a nearby lake. The challenger wriggled into a mighty, forty-foot-long water serpent with poisonous fangs, while Passamaquoddy's shaman got a bit more creative. He morphed into a huge *weewilmekq*, a giant, ferocious leech whose sharp, sucker-like mouth could latch onto something's skin and suck out its contents!

The two powerful beasts proceeded to battle. Their fighting churned the lake's waters, which locals say still chop violently to this day. Finally, after a terrible thrashing in the waters, a victor emerged. It was the leech, who had sucked his opponent dry, leaving the opposing shaman as nothing more than a powerless, hollowed-out shell.

This chapter has shown us that the collection of dragon serpents, worms, and leeches is not much different than the dark, fire-breathing dragons we explored earlier. Most are evil and embody humanity's worst qualities. But ancient stories tell us that there are many other kinds of dragons, including mighty beasts that could puff out clouds and spit rain. When they sparred, they sent blazing thunderbolts across the sky. While these dragons could wage war with weather, they could also light up the skies with radiant beauty.

CHAPTER TWO

FORCES OF NATURE

". . . the shock of my tail a thunderbolt, my wings a
hurricane, and my breath death!" —Smaug the dragon,
from J. R. R. Tolkien's *The Hobbit*

As many ancient cultures saw it, dragons and other serpent-like beasts were weather makers. They controlled precious rains and the flow of rivers. Their glowing eyes flashed lightning strikes; their beating wings unleashed lashing winds and tornadoes. Huge, flying dragons blocked portions of the sun and caused solar eclipses as a result. Special sea dragons conducted the ocean tides.

With Mother Nature gripped firmly in their talons, these dragons had the power to cause death and despair. And no beast was more feared for controlling vital rainfall and inflicting famine than India's legendary dragon, Vritra.

DROUGHT DEMON

Thousands of years ago—at least dating back to 1200 BCE—the people of India sang about an evil, snakelike dragon that was so massive, it could coil itself around mountains. Even more devastating, Vritra (which means "enveloper" in Sanskrit) had issues with water—*big* issues. The scaly control freak bottled up in its belly ALL of India's rivers and streams. It also wouldn't let a single drop of rain fall on the parched land. In time, crops withered. The earth blistered and cracked. People died.

Then a hero emerged. Indra, who would one day become king of the gods, knew he had to battle Vritra to save his homeland. After he mustered up a pair of thunderbolts (always helpful in battle!) and gulped down a special drink made from plants, Indra went to challenge Vritra. He lunged at the beast, but the dragon, quick and well-prepared, struck back. It seized Indra and began wrapping the man in its constricting coils. Then, quite unexpectedly, Vritra's grip softened, and the demon, according to one version of the tale, grew misty-eyed! Apparently, the beast (proving that dragons have feelings, too!) realized its evil ways and was ready to accept death. With his enemy now vulnerable, Indra threw a thunderbolt at Vritra's heart. Instantly, the dragon burst open, and all the pent-up rivers and streams gushed forth madly. It wasn't long before India flourished again.

CHINA'S GREAT RAIN DRAGON

In Chinese mythology, the dragon is generally considered a good and powerful creature. Many dragons exist in this culture (some of which we'll discuss in the next chapter), but here we'll mention Ying Long, which is also known as the rain dragon. This mighty creature shows up in quite a few ancient stories. In one, he blows out clouds and provides precious rain to a community stricken by drought.

In another, Ying Long helps the legendary ruler Yu the Great cope with TOO much water. Likely a mythical figure, Yu is believed to have started the Xia dynasty, the very first dynasty in Chinese history. (So, this is going back a long time ago, to about 2070-1600 BCE!) Yu becomes distraught when a massive flood—the Great Deluge—threatens the lives of his people, causing them to flee to hills, mountaintops, and the tops of trees.

Then the water-wise dragon Ying Long glides in. Tracing his tail across the land, he shows Yu where to dig canals that will help drain water away from the villages. The people are saved, and, in the process, learn about flood control and irrigation!

Numerous other legends from around the world feature dragons that control wind, water, and other weather events. One creature of importance to the Incas of Peru was the powerful *amaru*. This two-headed, serpent-like dragon (whose heads, by the way, sometimes resembled llamas or pumas!) was probably inspired by that region's notorious fat

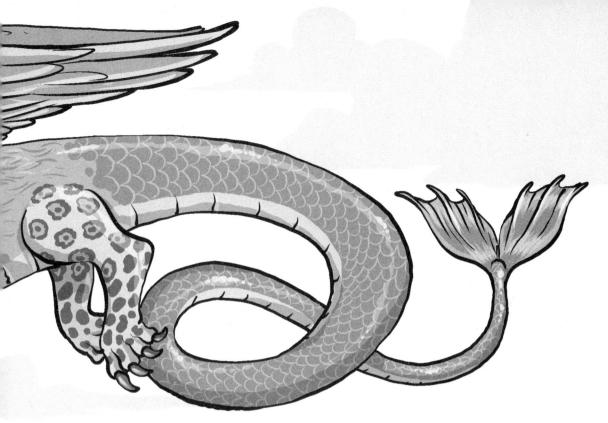

slider, the anaconda. In ancient times, an Incan leader once stocked a local prison with jaguars and amarus and determined that criminals who managed to survive the beasts for a period of three days could be set free. But amarus had glowing qualities, too. When this creature sucked water from a spring and shot it across the sky to another location, it caused a stunning a rainbow.

The Aborigines, Australia's earliest residents, also believed in a rainbow-making dragon they called the Rainbow Serpent. And according to natives of the Caribbean, there's a dragon with a powerful blowhole called Huracan. As you might have guessed, this blustery beast is often blamed for causing hurricanes!

These beasts have great powers, capable of changing the seasons and the weather. But what about dragons so precious that they spawned human life? Dragons associated with royalty, fortune, happiness? We'll meet them next.

CHAPTER THREE

DIVINE DRAGONS

"The dragon teaches you that if you want to climb high,
you have to do it against the wind." —Chinese proverb

Put down your sword and lance. It's time to kneel before the mighty dragon.

The scaly creatures we'll learn about next are a far cry (make that ROAR!) from the giant, child-eating reptiles we discussed earlier. In fact, in many of the tales that follow, you'll see that the dragon is not the villain, but the "saint" or hero of the story. Across the world, numerous cultures and peoples have a soft spot for dragons—beasts, as they see it, that represent peace, strength, wholeness, good luck, and more.

Chinese legends, for example, tell us that humans owe our very existence to this wise and powerful creature. In fact, many of the people of China consider themselves to be "descendants of the dragon" because to them, the dragon is the source of all energy and life.

The Chinese dragon is a bright, colorful, and lively creature, a far cry from the dark, venomous fire-breather of European lore! It can be found in art and culture all over China—from books, paintings, jewelry, and architecture to celebrations and events, such as the dragon dance and the Dragon Boat Festival.

Basically, the dragon is king in China (oops, that should be *emperor*)! Let's learn more about its fascinating origins.

A GOOD AND GENTLE BEAST IS BORN

According to legend, China's first people lived peacefully across their diverse and beautiful land. Different tribes occupied different parts of the country and sought the guidance of animals unique to their region.

The tribe that lived by the ocean revered the fish, which was agile. The tribe that lived in the mountains prized the lofty bird, which could chase the clouds away. Those that lived in the low plains cherished the horse, which could gallop at top speed. Those in the

high plains worshiped the serpent, which was silent and clever. And finally, the hard workers of the rice fields treasured the ox, which was strong and steady.

Over time, however, jealousies grew. Tribes envied one another for their powerful creatures. Tensions grew and fights erupted. War broke out across the land. Yet the children of the tribes were bewildered. *Why such violence? Why war?* they wondered. So, they forged a solution: They would create an animal that united all of China.

For the body of the creature, the children chose the serpent. This made the animal cunning. Onto the serpent, they glued the scales of the fish, to make the beast flexible. For the head, the children chose the horse, to make the creature fast. Onto the head, they attached the ox's horns, to make the beast strong. Finally, they added wings from the bird, to make the creature free.

The children's magnificent creation—a dragon—captivated the warring tribes. The adults vowed never again to go to war. And while the vow didn't stick, and battles occurred from time to time, the dragon always remained a symbol of both power and peace.

AN ANCIENT SO TREASURED

In terms of their age, dragons are the oldest legendary beasts. In China, archaeologists have found clay pots with dragon images on them that date back to around 5000 BCE (or about 7,000 years ago)! Scientists have also uncovered ancient dragon mosaics made from clamshells, as well as pieces of carved jade—beautifully colored stones typically green or bluish-green in color—in the shapes of dragons inside the tombs of Chinese kings and other nobility. Such jade pieces, which were carved into coiling shapes that resembled dragons, were probably used as pendants and might have been attached to a person's body or their clothing.

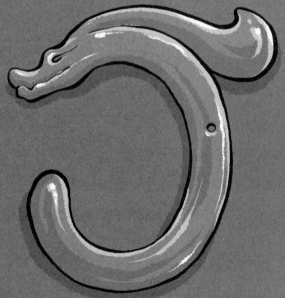

BEAST WITH A BEAT

Chinese New Year, or Spring Festival, is an important holiday in China. Traditionally, it's a time to honor deities and ancestors, but it's also associated with a variety of lighthearted activities. Delicious dumplings, cheerful red lanterns hung on doors, and late-night fireworks are all festive elements of the celebrations, and so are dragons—specifically, dancing dragons.

While the earliest dragon dances were serious affairs in which drought-stricken villages danced in desperation to beg the gods for rain, today these performances are decidedly fun. A team of dancers moves an extensive dragon form by holding up a series of poles attached to it. Experienced dancers (there are competitions!) can make a dragon move quite realistically, as if it were gliding through the air.

OTHER REVERED REPTILES

Dragons are sacred animals across Asia. In China, the creature is generally known as *lóng*; in Japan, *tatsu*; and in Korea, *yong*. Associated with rivers and seas, dragons were viewed as life-giving. They could harness the waters needed to farm and grow crops, the basis for any successful civilization.

In Japan, dragons are so sacred that sculptures and other images of them adorn many Buddhist temples and holy shrines. (Buddhism, which originated in ancient India, is a religion based on the teachings of the wise sage Gautama Buddha). And according to Korean legend, dragons can speak and experience emotions like kindness and devotion.

Surprisingly, serpents or snakes—generally loathed by many modern societies—were venerated across the ancient world. In India, the *nāga* is a spirit that can exist as a king cobra or a man. In one legend, Buddha, the great teacher and founder of Buddhism, was trying to meditate when hard rains began to pelt him. The cobra offered Buddha his hood and kept him dry.

The Greeks and Romans were so fond of snakes that they kept nonpoisonous ones as pets to protect their pantries from rats and mice! The speedy messenger and Greek god Hermes carried a rod entwined with two snakes, called a caduceus. We sometimes see this symbol today in connection to medicine and doctors' offices.

And you might think again when you see your silly pooch chasing his tail. The image of a dragon eating its tail was once a powerful symbol in ancient Egypt, which then spread to other cultures. Known as *ouroboros* (pronounced "yer-uh-BOR-us"), this ever-circling dragon, or serpent, was seen as self-reliant and persistent—one that never gives up. Could it be your symbol, too?

A FINE, FEATHERED DRAGON

Dragons were also sacred to the people of ancient Mexico and Central America. One with bright green feathers and a long, flowing tail was thought to blaze across the sky. Part-dragon, part-bird and really fun to say, Quetzalcóatl (pronounced "kwet-zuh-kwatl") was an important god to people living in early Mexico and Central America.

It's quite possible, too, that Quetzalcóatl was a real person. This Aztec leader was said to help civilize his people by denouncing barbaric practices such as human sacrifice. And while he okayed the sacrifice of some small creatures, including "large grasshoppers" (which still seems cruel!), it was a vast improvement over people killing their neighbors in the name of the gods!

Because Quetzalcóatl was rebelling against the old ways, it wasn't long before he attracted an enemy. This mythical figure, Tezcatlipoca, was associated with a god known for darkness and trickery. He wished to destroy Quetzalcóatl's empire, and using his best tricks and disguises, Tezcatlipoca killed many of its citizens. His most sneaky trap involved luring helpless citizens with the alluring aromas of freshly roasted corn (not fair!) and killing them.

According to the legend, a weary Quetzalcóatl fled to the sea, using the last of his powers to make a boat comprised of braided snakes. The Aztecs didn't give up hope, though, that one day their hero would return.

Years later, they thought that day had come when they spied a large fleet of ships on the horizon. But this was a tragic mistake. For it wasn't Quetzalcóatl who had returned to save them—it was Spanish conquistadors, who would eventually destroy the Aztec people and their way of life. At least the mythical Quetzalcóatl lives on to remind us of these people's once-vibrant culture.

Over the course of thousands of years, though, fascination with dragons and magical serpents started to wane. An increasingly modern and scientific world started to demand facts to back up these stories and legends—and ultimately to trap or net a real live, breathing dragon. While scientists and explorers have yet to find this legendary dragon in the flesh, what they have found may surprise you.

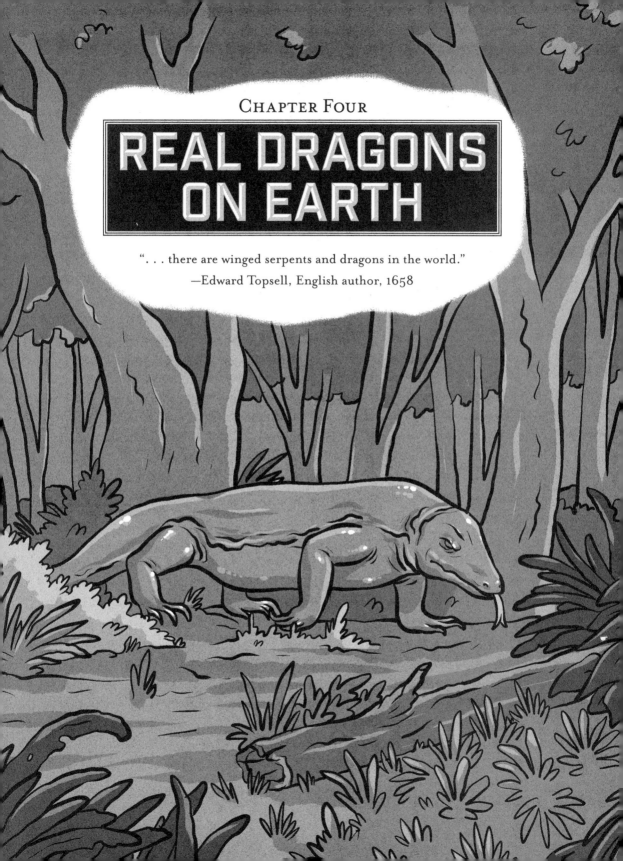

Chapter Four

REAL DRAGONS ON EARTH

". . . there are winged serpents and dragons in the world."
—Edward Topsell, English author, 1658

Dragons had sailed, slithered, and soared through so many cultural myths that by the eighteenth century, scientists were eager to find out if these fascinating beasts were actually real or simply the stuff of legends.

Varanus Komodoensis

One such dragon seeker was Swiss physician Johann Jakob Scheuchzer. Like other naturalists of the 1700s, Scheuchzer was happy to journey the globe in search of nature's dazzling life-forms. But the goal was serious and scientific: to identify, catalog, and organize all the living world's abundant diversity. Thanks to Carl Linnaeus, a Swedish zoologist, scientists now had a method for naming these varied organisms—with each organism receiving two names, a genus and a species. Hard to pronounce, these names are usually written in Latin, the language used by the world's first scholars and scientists.

Scheuchzer just happened to be drawn to the spectacular—and to dragons. (Can you blame him?) So in the early 1700s, he embarked on a dragon-hunting quest through the Alps of Switzerland. Along the way, he collected reports from people who swore they'd seen dragons, including one man who likened the flying fire-breathers to meteors flashing across the sky. But Scheuchzer never saw a single dragon or found any dragon evidence—bones, teeth, fossils, or anything else.

Serious men of science, like Linnaeus, had little tolerance for such a bizarre-sounding (and, even more importantly, undocumented) creature. Linnaeus refused to include dragons in his official catalog of living things known as *Systema Naturae*. He gave them a mention, however, under a category he termed *Paradoxa*, a group of unverifiable misfits that included the unicorn, the phoenix, and a creature known as the "giant tadpole."

BUT WHY SO MANY DRAGONS?

So how is it that the dragon repeatedly shows up in the myths and legends of cultures all over the world? Ancient peoples lived on different continents. They never knew one another or communicated with one another, yet still so many came up with the idea of a dragon. How?

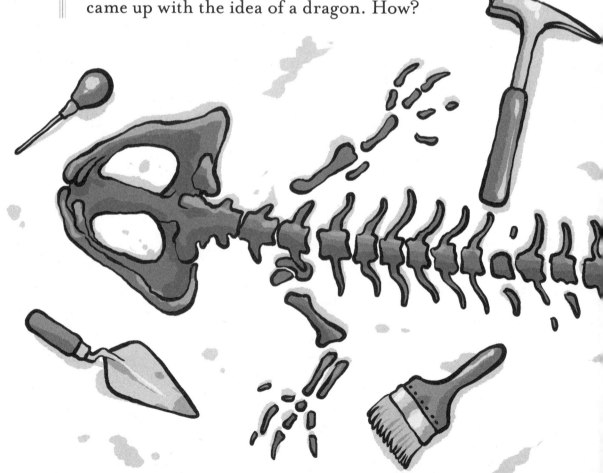

Let's go back to Scheuchzer for an explanation. During one of his many expeditions, Scheuchzer uncovered an unusual fossil that included a head attached to a three-foot-long skeleton. Based on a passage from the Old Testament of the Bible, he believed that he knew what he'd found. The skeleton was of a "wicked" man, he was convinced, who God had punished and drowned during the Great Flood.

Or was it?

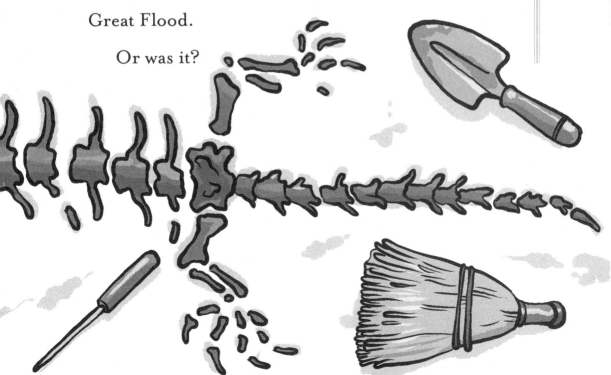

Fast forward to 1811 (eighty years after Scheuchzer's death). The French anatomist Georges Cuvier, also known as the "Father of Paleontology," examined Scheuchzer's stunning fossil and discovered that the dragon dreamer was sadly mistaken. The fossil was not of a man, or of any human (evil, good, or otherwise). The fossil was of an ichthyosaur, a reptile that lived millions of years ago!

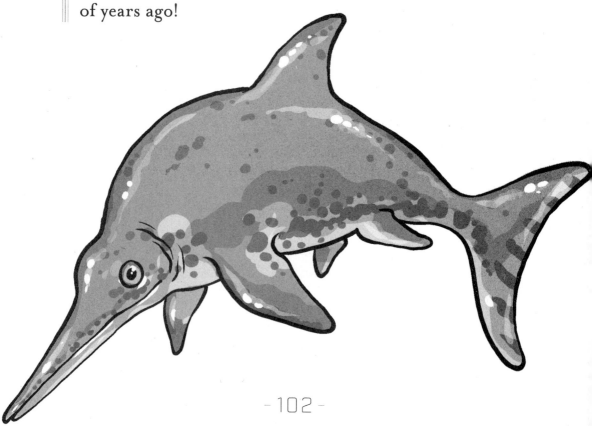

Fossils, as you can see, were quite mysterious. And if early scientists could interpret them incorrectly, there was a good chance that ordinary people, with little or no scientific training, could get them wrong too. Just like Scheuchzer, it's likely that early peoples who stumbled across strange bones and fossils formulated their own ideas about the creatures to which they belonged. (To be fair, today, Scheuchzer is considered an important founder of paleobiology. He was hardly the first scientist of his era to confuse myth with reality!) Early people envisioned a beast with a large reptilian body, sharp teeth, and claws and called it a *dragon*. We see those same features today, often in a museum, and call this creature by another name: *dinosaur*!

NIGHTMARES? BLAME EARLY MAMMALS

Our early ancestors made a mistake. They saw dino bones, and oops—dragons came to mind! But another explanation for the abundance of dragon tales is not our fault. You see, the brains that we inherited, following millions of years of evolution, came preprogrammed (like a toy loaded with batteries and ready to play) with several features. One of these, passed along by our genes, was fear—specifically, a fear of deadly predators. Think pouncing panthers with blazing eyes. Large raptor birds with flesh-tearing claws. Oversized crocodiles with large, jutting teeth. Early mammals learned to bolt or seek shelter in response to these stealthy, aggressive creatures.

This fear response, which saved these soft and furry animals' backs, became hardwired into the mammalian brain. Eventually, modern humans (we're animals, too!) inherited this fear. This likely explains our instinctive fear of snakes, other reptiles, and large birds. It also helps explain why children who've never even seen a snake can sometimes report having nightmares about them! Such fears may have also laid the foundation for our concept of the dragon. The dragon, especially the western dragon, is the ultimate scary predator—a combination of all deadly predators combined!

EVEN BETTER THAN DRAGONS?

It's true that real dragons likely never existed. But that doesn't mean we have to stop enjoying them—or the powerful ideas that they symbolize. It's also true that the planet abounds with real, live creatures that might seem even *more* fantastic than dragons.

Let's consider a lizard that can reach ten feet long and weigh as much as 360 pounds. It's burly and stocky, and has jaws built for devouring massive amounts of meat. Outfitted with a special hinge, its lower jaw can pop open extra wide, allowing for enormous bites. And its stomach stretches easily, enabling it to eat up to eighty percent of its own body weight in a single meal!

hinged lower jaw

can eat 80% of its
body weight at once

stretchy
stomach

can grow up
to 10 feet long

can get up to 360 pounds

Any guesses on what this "dragon" is? It's the largest lizard on earth, the Komodo dragon. Found on the islands of Indonesia, Komodo dragons eat whole pigs, deer, and water buffalo. While these dragons can't fly or breathe fire, they do possess some spectacular (and disgusting) quirks. For one, if a feasting Komodo needs to flee in a hurry, it can regurgitate (or throw up)

its meal! Another thing: The dragon's teeth are covered with germs, including some that can kill if exposed to other creatures. Since the lizard eats dead, rotting meat frequently, a residue builds up on its teeth. Within these grooves and gunk, numerous species of bacteria grow. At least fifty kinds have been identified by scientists! Talk about dragon breath!

There are several other dragon-like creatures. One is the bearded dragon, which flares its impressive spiky "beard" if it feels threatened. Not only can these Australian lizards puff out their necks, they can also change color throughout the day. Turning lighter in color as the sun grows hotter might help the lizard optimize heat absorption.

Bearded Dragon

And yes, there really is a flying dragon in nature! Living in the tropical forests of Southeast Asia, the flying dragon lizards (classified under the genus *Draco*) can glide through the air, thanks to a unique body design that includes extra-long, lightweight ribs.

Flying Dragon Lizard

Like mythical dragons, there are also living "dragons" associated with the oceans. Dragonets are tropical fish found in the Indian and Pacific Oceans that sport large, frilly fins. These fish can be drab in color or a mix of gaudy bright blue, orange, and yellow. While dragonets are the graceful dragons of the sea, dragonfish are decidedly grotesque. With needle-sharp fangs that protrude from their mouths, these scary-looking fish boast a weird accessory for nabbing a meal. Called a barbel, a long stem of flesh with a glowing tip hangs from the fish's chin and acts as a lure. Smaller fish are drawn to the natural glow, or bioluminescence, coming from the dragonfish's barbel, and are then snapped up by it.

Other dragon-like creatures here on Earth include sea dragons, dragon snakes, dragon millipedes, and, of course, dragonflies!

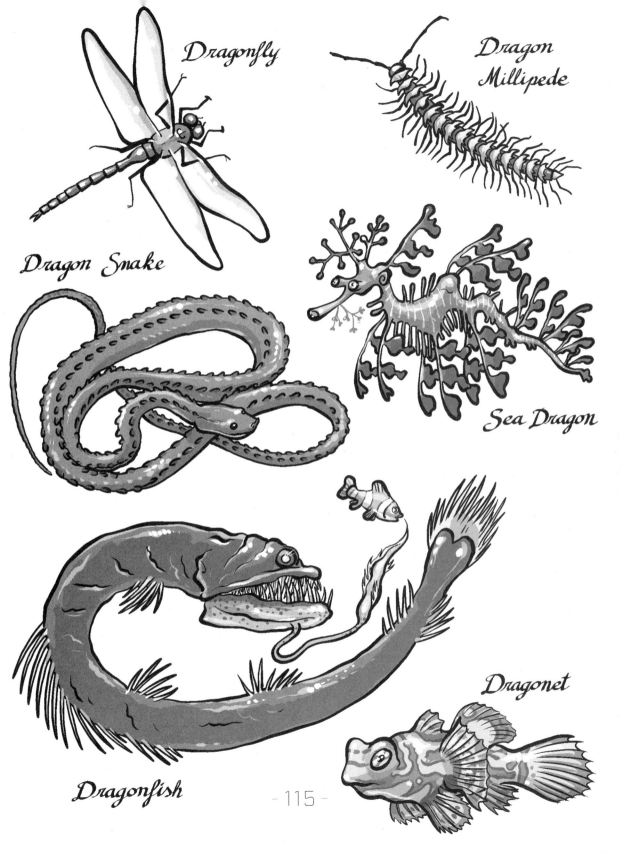

Dragonfly

Dragon Millipede

Dragon Snake

Sea Dragon

Dragonet

Dragonfish

THE MANY SCALES OF A DRAGON

"The hunger of a dragon is slow to wake, but hard to sate."
—Ursula K. Le Guin, *A Wizard of Earthsea*

As we've learned, mythical dragons are not simple creatures. They're not entirely evil. They're not angelic little fire-breathers, either! We see their complex personalities come to life in numerous pop culture characters from Disney's Maleficent (*Sleeping Beauty*) and Mushu (*Mulan*), to Dragon (*Shrek*) and Elliott (*Pete's Dragon*).

The Chinese believe that the dragon possesses 117 scales. Eighty-one of these are associated with goodness and light. Thirty-six are associated with negative energy. Complex, often misunderstood and yearning, with a host of faults, to find a place in the world—aren't we all a little like dragons?

Main Sources

Johnsgard, Paul, and Karin Johnsgard. *Dragons and Unicorns: A Natural History*. New York: St. Martin's Press, 1982.

Jones, David E. *An Instinct for Dragons*. New York: Routledge, 2002.

Passes, David. *Dragons: Truth, Myth, and Legend*. New York: Western Publishing Company, 1993.

Rose, Carol. *Giants, Monsters, and Dragons: An Encyclopedia of Folklore, Legend, and Myth*. New York: W. W. Norton & Company, 2001.

Shuker, Karl. *Dragons: A Natural History*. New York: Simon & Schuster, 1995.

Tolkien, J. R. R. *Beowulf: A Translation and Commentary*. New York: Houghton Mifflin, 2014.

For Further Reading

Dragons might be mythical beasts, but you can keep them alive in your imagination. Check out these titles—or ask a librarian for suggestions—to keep your inner dragon fire burning!

- *Dealing with Dragons* by Patricia C. Wrede
- *Dragon Keeper* by Carole Wilkinson
- *Dragon Rider* by Cornelia Funke
- *Dragon's Nest* by Emily Rodda
- *Eragon* by Christopher Paolini
- *Falcon's Egg* by Luli Gray
- *Hatching Magic* by Ann Downer
- *The Hobbit* by J. R. R. Tolkien